Kid's Guide to Water Formations

Children's Science & Nature

BABY PROFESSOR

EDUCATION KIDS

Speedy Publishing LLC
40 E. Main St. #1156
Newark, DE 19711
www.speedypublishing.com

There are different water formations that we can see or even experience. Their names are based on how they look, their depth and breadth, whether the water is fresh or salty, and whether the water is flowing or not. Let's get to know each water formation.

Coves

A cove is a
sheltered area
along the shoreline
of a large body
of water, where
the water gathers.
When the main
body of water is
very active, the
water in the cove
may be calmer.

Bay

A bay is like
a cove but is
rather larger.

Gulfs

These are a large portion of a sea or ocean that are partially surrounded by land. To help you understand this idea, look at a map of the Gulf of Mexico. It is connected to the Atlantic Ocean, but is partly surrounded by North and Central America.

Lakes

A lake is a large body of water that is surrounded by land on all sides. Water in lakes is colder at the top during the summer. Lakes usually hold fresh water, but there are some salt-water lakes.

Ponds

A pond also surrounded on all sides by land, however, it has less water and is a smaller size. Whether a body of water like this is called a lake or a pond depends a lot on local customs. Water in ponds has same temperature throughout.

Rivers

A river is a larger body of water that flows above the ground from a higher elevation down toward sea level. Rivers always have more water in it than streams do. Rivers usually flow to other bodies of water. For example, the water from the Mississippi River flows into the Gulf of Mexico.

Sea

A sea is a large body of salt water that is surrounded by land or it can be attached to another body of water. An example of a sea surrounded by land is The Caspian Sea.

Oceans

An ocean, which is the largest body of water on Earth, is generally considered as having no boundaries. You can just locate them based on the nearby landmass or continents. All oceans have salt water

Now that you know these different water forms, you can be identify the bodies of water when you see them on a map, or when you are traveling.

These are the most common names for the major water formations. You may learn other, more local names— for instance, in Scotland a lake is a "loch". In northern Europe, a bay can be a "fjord".

Visit

BABY PROFESSOR
EDUCATION KIDS

www.BabyProfessorBooks.com

to download Free Baby Professor eBooks
and view our catalog of new and exciting
Children's Books

CPSIA information can be obtained
at www.ICGtesting.com
Printed in the USA
BVHW060835290722
643138BV00005B/444

9 781541 903807